ISBN 978-0-9978175-3-9

Printed in the United States of America

Avatars & Drones

Warren Dent

Acknowledgments

My writing group has been a constant source of review and critique on several of the stories contained in this collection. I thank them for their insistence on 'showing', not 'telling' wherever possible.

My wife, Gail Monica, has put up with incomplete, misspelled, and poorly expressed first drafts, and has energetically Americanized strange Australian expressions and idioms.

Thanks to all.

Author's Note

There are four short stories here. My definition of a short story is one that is between 1,500 and 10,000 words.

This is an eclectic mix of tales with no full uniting theme. Three of them are mild science fiction tales, the fourth is a technology mystery. They are first attempts at writing in new genres, so please be patient and forgiving. One sci-fi story is the shortest at under 2,000 words. The technology mystery is two and a half times as long. Be prepared for a wide variety in subject matter, style, and length, and enjoy the new creativity.

You can find my website at www.krandis.com. My email address is warren@krandis.com

Avatars & Drones

Warren Dent

Table of Stories

Two boys and their Toy

Chapter 1

As the cab swung to the curb, Ron reached back and withdrew his battered billfold from his rear pants' pocket. The cab stopped and the driver turned towards his passenger. Ron flipped his wallet open and let his fingers probe the note compartment to extract payment. The only thing he encountered however was the soft, thin leather membrane divider.

"What the heck?" he muttered. He checked the car seat to see if his money had slipped out somehow. No luck.

Addressing the cabbie, he said "No cash. Sorry. Can you take a credit card?"

The driver scowled, grumbled, "Yes, but there'll be a $5 surcharge," and attached the card-slide to his cellphone. Ron handed over a credit card and squiggled his initials across the screen of the driver's phone to approve the charge.

Inside his work cubicle, before even switching on his office computer, he called his wife, at home. "Hi Beth, glad I caught you."

Beth had her purse in her hand and was heading for the front door. She responded breathlessly, "Hi hon, what's up? I'm about to leave."

"Did I leave any cash anywhere in the kitchen this morning, or give you money last night? I had over $300 in my wallet yesterday but it seems to be gone. Had to use a credit card to pay the cab."

"Well, you didn't give me any funds, that's for sure, sweetheart. Let me double check the table and counters. I haven't had time to clear them this morning."

Beth retreated to the kitchen and looked around. Back on the phone, her tone was apologetic. "Nothing here Ron. You didn't blow it on booze or chicks last night did you? I was already in bed when you finally got home."

"Right. You fink." He smiles. "I guess that gal must have cost more than I remember. I'll try and find her again tonight. Wonder where that money went."

Chapter 2

The machine parts Pete had disassembled lay scattered across the basement table, surrounding the main plastic superstructure frame.

"There, that's the last wireless hookup activated," Doug muttered. "What are the diagnostics showing now?"

Pete whipped around the old wooden table to get a straight-on view of the laptop. "Hmmm, the gyroscope on strut four is out of position. Obviously providing false proximity info to the other three scopes and confusing the system's balance perception. No wonder we've had some fetch problems. Scope must have gotten knocked somehow."

"Yeah, but more importantly, can we fix it?"

Ever the optimist, and more responsive to challenges, Pete responds, "Gonna have a go, in any event. Shouldn't be too difficult. I'll pull up the user manual online and see what it says."

An hour later, the machine is declared fit to use by its maintenance system, so Doug plugs the power cable into the fast-charge wall socket and begins recharging. "Sure glad we bought the model with the patented Musk-brand batteries, they give us so much more time. And they recharge much faster than the old ones. Come on, let's go play SpaceInvader for an hour. We're all set for tonight, right?"

Chapter 3

Glenys welcomed the five ladies with open emotion. "Thank you so much, all of you, for coming. I was dreading doing this with just two of us. Father O'Brien says they are expecting over 50 women tonight. The topic sounds a bit too embarrassing for me, so I'm glad to be back here preparing the food."

Andrea speaks up with conviction. "Well, I was fortunate to hear Dr. Andrews give this speech six months ago. Let me tell you, she's very good. And I don't mind saying I learned some stuff I thought I knew, but turns out my information was erroneous. Wish I'd known more before Graham died of cancer so early. Might have managed a few more orgasms before he was gone."

An awkward hush falls over the small group. Glenys harrumphs. "I don't believe you need to share any more, Andrea. Let's talk about what we've got to organize for the buffet dinner tonight." A couple of audible snickers reveal not everyone is ready yet to move on. But Glenys persists. "You can put your coats and handbags in the storage room ladies. Hope you all brought your own aprons as there's no extras here. Pots and pans, skillets, tongs, all the necessary kitchen plates, glasses and cutlery, but nothing personal for us preparers. Not even chefs' hats. Now, let's organize in teams of two..."

Chapter 4

Ron, who can't find $300, shoves his food around his plate, picking at the offerings. He and Beth are digesting take-out Chinese, although it's doubtful whether Ron can taste anything. For the life of him he cannot work out how the cash disappeared from his wallet. "I know I had six fifties and two twenties sitting in the back section of this beat-up hunk of leather." He waves it in front of his wife. "Here, Beth, you have a look. Are there any holes, or seams pulled apart through which the notes could have slipped out?"

Beth dutifully inspects the wallet, and declares, "Not that I can see, hon. Sure is a mystery. Are you sure you didn't take the cash out and hide it in a dresser drawer, knowing the cleaning ladies were coming this morning?"

"That's a fair thought, sweetheart. I did check when I got home, but perhaps your eyes will see something mine didn't if you take a look." Trying to offer a semblance of humor, he grins and adds, "I know how much you like your hand in my drawers."

Beth smirks. "Ha, you wish!" but leaves the table and heads upstairs.

She returns five minutes later holding up two $1 bills. "No $300 I'm afraid, but here's your secret savings cache. Probably from a time you did hide money under your socks."

"Well, thanks for checking, hon. Maybe this place has a ghost, like the landlord once implied when we moved in immediately after our marriage ten years ago. Ha. If we lived on the ground floor I'd suspect someone reached in the window and took it off the little table where we leave the house and car keys. But not here on the second floor. Maybe I'll buy a videocam on the weekend, and set it up to watch that window we leave open."

"I think you must have moved it to some other place for safekeeping, Ron, which you've now temporarily forgotten. It can't really just disappear by flying out the window can it? One of these days we'll find exactly where you left it. Come on. Our show starts in two minutes. Let's clean up here and go watch it. You'll just have to work some more overtime to buy that present for your girlfriend."

Chapter 5

At the edge of the park, Doug and Pete sit on a bench partially concealed from the main path by heavy shrubbery. Pete reaches down and eases the quadrasonic drone out of its protective casing. He adjusts the angle of the high res camera and locks the grab/snatch mechanism into position. Doug plugs one end of the long USB cable into the drone's belly and hands the other end to Pete who secures it in the front port on the laptop. The Highsky software starts up automatically and runs its pre-flight test sequence. Thirty seconds later a large green checkmark on the screen indicates all systems go.

Doug moves closer to Pete and they open and extend the craft's casing box to form a flat work table which they lay across their knees. With the batteries fully charged, Doug checks the quad controls, engages the motor, and elevates the machine six feet into the air. It's virtual noiselessness, which is one of the main reasons the boys chose this particular model. Pete links his tablet to the laptop and opens the camera and snatch control programs. A few simple maneuvers convince him the two components are working perfectly. "OK, Doug," he whispers, a giant grin covering his face. "Input the GPS coordinates I gave you and head east."

Using the Google map as a guide, Doug unerringly navigates the machine out of the park and along a back alley at a height of ten feet. He flies slowly and carefully, monitoring the various gauges and indicators for any signs of unusual engine performance or flight path deviations, but none occur. There is one major street to cross. He pauses the machine close to the wall of the brick building which forms the corner. Pete swings the camera to the left to watch the traffic lights at the nearby intersection. He waits patiently until they turn green. "You can go now," he tells Doug. Doug adds five feet to the lift and quickly crosses the road. Most drivers in the cars below are busy focusing on the traffic lights and the drone's progress is undetected. The main portion of the Sacred Heart Church is to the left with the meeting hall beyond.

The boys tense.

Pete whispers, as if he's standing in the dark alleyway itself. "Let's see if that window above the back door is still open. Slowly, ever so slowly, Doug. You're doing great."

Pete adjusts the camera angle. "There it is. Perfect. No-one has touched it."

Doug's hands start sweating. From here on, true precision flying is required. One small error and the adventure ends. He draws in a deep breath and holds it.

Chapter 6

Pete directs the camera straight ahead, focusing on the window aperture. "You're not quite centered Doug, move two inches to the right." The window is only a few inches wider than the drone. Doug barely touches the controls. "Perfect," Pete whispers. "Put her in hover mode and let's pause outside the window for a moment while I pull in the video signal from the webcam I installed earlier in the storage room. It'll take a few seconds to make the Bluetooth connection and link to the tablet. Ahhh, there we go!"

"What do you see bro'?"

"There are four, no, five ladies hanging up coats, two are now putting on aprons, one is changing her shoes. They're laughing at something. Whoops, another woman just entered and the others stopped laughing. They are trying to look serious, but one can't help herself. She's cracking up and the others are trying to hide grins. Wonder what that's all about?" Now, they're leaving and I can see their handbags bunched together on a small table."

"OK, let me have a look. Here you manage the hover controls for a few seconds. Wow, you set that web-cam camera up perfectly in that storage room Pete. How did you disguise it?"

"Ha, just piled some kids' religious books all around it on a high shelf after Sunday Fellowship last Monday. Of no interest to those ladies."

"Looks good. Give me back the controls. Time to move our hover-friend through the window and into the hallway. Come on little babe. Nice and steady. Even as you go. Be good for me."

With hands of steel Doug glides the drone through the narrow window into the back hallway of the church annex. The place is amazingly noisy, with 50 women gossiping and laughing nervously over their buffet dinner. The storage room is to the left, the kitchen to the right. Both doors are partially closed.

The boys smile at each other. Not a problem. To progress further just requires a little more dexterity and finesse.

It's Pete's turn. Deftly maneuvering the mouse on the tablet, he extends the telescopic snatch tool until its pincers protrude beyond the rotors. "OK, Doug, go."   Doug's adrenaline is pumping, but with a soft nudge, he forces the drone obliquely forward and the storage door hinges wide open. The boys pause and execute a quick high-five.

Pete smiles, and whoops, "Unbelievable. We're in, and no one is the wiser."

Pete rotates the camera in a 360 degree search pattern. "I see six large handbags on the table, two with pieces of paper sticking out. Let me look more closely." He extends the zoom lens, and quickly pulls back. "Damn, the first one is just a receipt. No go. Let me try the other one. Can you rotate the

machine about 90 degrees clockwise Doug? I might be able to see better."

Doug nudges the controls and the drone twirls firmly to the right. "Oh yes," Pete whispers. "Ten more degrees, slowly now."

Pete is intensely focused on the second bag. Suddenly, he turns to Doug and orders, "Stealth mode now!"

"What's up?" Doug responds, as the machine goes almost totally silent, using minimal power to stay aloft, ceasing all unnecessary functions.

"Shit, I thought I saw a shadow move across the floor by the doorway. Damn, damn, damn. Last thing we need is to be discovered by someone as we raid these handbags. OK, let's check. Re-activate the main camera for me. We may have to get out of there."

Doug powers the machine back up and Pete rotates the camera lens. "Shit, there we go. It was a cat. He's laying down outside the kitchen door now. Must keep the church free of rats. Whew, thank heavens it wasn't a helper or janitor or an attendee even. That was scary. OK, back to the task at hand. Let me get back to zooming in on that big bag."

Doug brings the machine up to full function again. "What are you seeing Pete? Anything worthwhile?"

"I think we've hit the jackpot Doug. This enormous black tote is gaping open at the top. On the inside of one side there is a zippered pouch. Maybe nine inches long, and four inches deep. And if you can believe it, it's unzipped. A very careless owner, for I see a bunch of cash in there. Hold steady buddy while I use the snatch device. This will be a bit tricky."

Both boys hold their breath as Pete cautiously proceeds. Doug doesn't dare speak and interrupt Pete's concentration, but waits anxiously. After a minute, Pete turns and smiles at his partner. "Got the whole stash buddy. Let me retract the hook, while you get ready to depart. There, done. Can't wait to see how much we got. All yours now, back to base please, maestro."

Chapter 7

Dr. Andrews finishes her talk on Women's Sexuality, and bows graciously in acknowledgment of the enthusiastic applause her audience provides. Andrea whispers to Glenys. "See what I mean? They love her. She's so friendly and down-to-earth. And I bet, if you are honest with yourself, that you learned something new. Yes?"

"I thought the talk was gross Andrea. That stuff shouldn't be talked about in public. I played solitaire on my cellphone for most of the time."

"Oh dear, you're far more prudish than I thought. Too bad."

"Somethings should remain private in my view. But in any event, I do thank you for coming along tonight. You were a powerhouse of help with the dinner arrangements and cleanup, doing far more than anyone else."

"I enjoyed the whole evening Glenys. Sorry you didn't. I just wish there'd been more time to get to know your other helpers. I see they've gone already."

"I'm indebted to you Andrea. Thanks again. I think we can just exit along with everyone else. The janitor has arrived, and we can leave him to tidy up further. I need to visit the ladies room, so I'll be in touch later. Bye."

Chapter 8

"This is unbelievable bro'. There's twelve hundred dollars here. Why would any woman carry that much money in her handbag? Can you imagine how pissed she's going to be when she finds it missing? I almost feel guilty. But I'm damned if we're going to give any of it back."

"I'm with you, Pete" Doug responds. "But we need to get out of here before someone calls the cops."

"How much have we made?" Pete asks.

"Counting the $300 yesterday, we're at $2600. But we need to lay low for a while, and not get greedy. If all those folks who lost funds went to the cops, a good detective may recognize a pattern."

Pete hesitates. "Yep, I have another idea we could try. Let's head back, and I'll tell you about it."

Chapter 9

Glenys turned out the bedside light, rolled onto her left side, and closed her eyes. That Andrea sure was a reliable friend. Glenys shuffled a couple of times to find the right position, and had happily settled when her cellphone rang. The screen showed Andrea's name, and as much as Glenys wanted to let the call go to voicemail, she answered cheerily.

"Andrea, have you been sharing more of Dr. Andrew's suggestions with your daughters? What do they think?"

"No Glenys," the tone serious, "Unfortunately I have a little problem. The girls will have to wait. Can I ask you how much you know about the other four helpers at tonight's event?"

"Why, what's up Andrea?"

"I'll tell you in a minute. Did you invite them all personally, or did some volunteer out of the blue when the notice went out?"

"I've known them all for years. They're trusted friends."

"Well, I'm short a bunch of cash that was in my handbag. I went to give it to hubby when I got home, and it was gone."

"Oh dear, how much are we talking about Andrea?"

"$1200. It was to be part of a birthday present for Jack to go buy new skis and boots. It's his birthday next week, and he likes to choose his own things. I'm devastated."

"And you think one of my friends helped themselves to your money?"

"I don't see who else would have had access to the storage room Glenys. Do you?"

"No, not immediately. This is terrible. I'm awfully sorry. I'd trust my friends with my life. I've never had any doubts about their honesty. Are you sure about the money being in your bag when you left it in the storage room?"

"Absolutely. While I hate to cast aspersions, that cash is definitely gone. I have the ATM receipts to show two withdrawals, and Jack saw me reach into the pouch in my handbag. *Let's face it Glenys, one of your friends is a low-down thief. Since you invited them along, you need to fix this, or I'm going to the police!*"

Glenys recoils at the vehemence, holds the phone away from her ear, and hangs up.

Chapter 10

"Here's my idea Doug. More and more people are ordering goods online these days and having them delivered by UPS. UPS is so busy that they are advertising for more drivers. As I've bicycled around the neighborhood I've seen lots of Amazon and other parcels sitting on front porches waiting to be picked up. Not everyone checks every day for parcels. But we could."

"I don't get it. Check what, how?"

"Come on Doug, you're being a bit thick, dummy. If there's a small parcel sitting out overnight, we could go pick it up and take whatever's inside – if it's something useful. I don't know what percent of such parcels would have anything valuable, but we sure could experiment and find out. What do you think?"

"You are so smart Pete. Great idea, although more work than picking wallets and handbags. I think we'd be throwing a bunch of stuff away that we don't want. We'll need a stronger snatch hook to pick up parcels heavier and bulkier than cash. I'll get onto researching options this afternoon. This could be fun."

Chapter 11

Detective Ben Johnson shakes his head.   This was the sixth call in two weeks about parcels being stolen from a front porch. The callers all had the same story. UPS deliveries were going missing.

Ben surmises that neighborhood kids riding bicycles are the culprits. If bigger articles had disappeared it could be someone in a car.   But bigger boxes would be too awkward to carry around on a bike, so the kids concentrate on smaller articles.

Ben turns to his partner Paul. "Ordinarily these thefts wouldn't be worth pursuing, but one of those callers was the mayor. I suppose all we can do is put out extra patrols in the area, say between 11pm to 3am, and have the officers look for anyone riding a bike. Do you think kids would be out later than that?"

Paul strokes his chin. "I think that's a good starting point Ben. The map pinpointing these thefts is pretty large however. And there are probably more thefts that folks haven't reported. We might want a couple of cars out at the same time, so if the kids see one and hide, they'll think they are clear. The second one may catch them."

"OK, I'll set up an initial effort for two weeks starting tomorrow. Even if we don't catch anyone, the presence of the cars may just be enough to stop kids from even setting out on their bikes. Let's keep track of any more calls about stolen deliveries."

"You got it Bud. I'll tell the Captain to let the mayor know our plan."

Chapter 12

"This is our best night's haul so far Pete. Seven 'reward boxes'. Let's hope there's something in them we can actually use. I'm tired of toothpaste, garden gloves, girls' panties, baseball cards, silver spoons and photo frames. Heck, the only worthwhile things so far are the cookies and two porn DVDs. Maybe the good stuff is in bigger boxes that are too heavy for the drone."

"Yep, not as valuable as I had hoped, I must admit, Doug. And I do worry about being caught. Surely if enough people complain about their losses, either UPS or the cops will do something about it. Here, you open these four parcels, I'll do the other three."

"OK. First box. What on earth is this? Two giant tubes. Yuk, throw-up medicine for cats. Good riddance. Let me try box number two. At least it's not an Amazon delivery."

"No delivery name anywhere? Weird."

"Uh, oh, Pete, it's a small handgun with 5 bullets in a plastic sleeve. This is scary shit. What the fuck do we do?"

"Oh boy. We have to get rid of this fast Doug. Scary ain't the right word. We get caught with this we're in serious, serious trouble. Guess we could try and throw it away somewhere, but if ever traced back to us we'll be skinned alive."

"Shit, shit shit. I'm willing to bet this is illegal. Look, there's no registration or license documentation. This is worse than we thought. How would we explain that away?"

Pete scratches his head. "I know. Let's pack it up and deliver it back to where we found it. We want nothing to do with this buddy. You work on repacking the box as close as you can to how it arrived, while I see if there's any other bad stuff in the remainder of our haul."

Chapter 13

Pete opens the remaining five boxes. "Nothing scary here Doug. Thank heavens. We can toss everything except two credit cards we picked up. Two cards for $350 each for the Richardson daughters according to the attached card. Really nice birthday gifts, apparently from their grandma and grandpa. Clearly loving, trusting folks because these cards are pre-activated to make it easy for the girls. Big mistake. We'll be able to buy whatever we need."

"Good deal. I've got this weapon packed. Looks like it did when delivered. Let's go put it back."

"You bet. I checked the address. Half a block from the house there's a road bridge over a little creek. Why don't we manage the drone from under there?"

"Once we get it back in place, Pete, we should let the police know anonymously about its existence. I've got one of those throw-away pre-paid cell phones. Maybe I could purchase a replacement afterwards using one of those credit cards we found tonight. OK by you?"

"No problem. Good thinking."

As the boys prop their bikes against the bridge abutment, Pete grabs Doug's jacket and pulls him into the shadows. "Shit, that was a cop car turning at the intersection a block away. Quick, let's pull the bikes under the bridge where they can't be seen, and wait a bit."

Doug whispers. "This is just too fucking scary Pete. I don't think I want to do this anymore after tonight."

"Yeah, I beginning to feel the same way. Shhh. Let's wait five minutes 'til the cops disappear from the area."

Chapter 14

Detectives Ben and Paul walk out of interrogation room P-5, both with big smiles. Ben turns to his partner and they shake hands. "One more illegal weapon off the streets. One more citizen with unknown intentions added to our firearms watch database. And all because of an anonymous tip. I swear that voice sounded familiar. I just can't place it. Maybe it will come to me later. Come on my friend, my treat for lunch today."

"Yes sirree! I bet the tip came from the kids who have been stealing the boxes in the neighborhood. They must have opened the package and sealed it back up and replaced it. No fingerprints anywhere. Think they've been learning about police procedures from all those cop shows on TV?"

Ben pushes open the front doors of the station and pauses on the top step.

"You know, maybe there's some goodness in those kids after all. I usually don't take home any of my cases, but I think this is one I can share tonight with my boys."

"I wish my daughters were as responsible as your sons, Ben. Doug and Pete are the best. I'm sure they'll appreciate your story."

Goodbye Again

The keyboard vibrates as the lights under the mechanical keys change from blue to red, and a hollow female voice rises from the embedded speaker. "Hi Roger. I saw you were home, thought I'd catch up with you."

"This is an important video I'm working on Julia, I hope you saved it when you interrupted."

"Of course I did. Haven't I always looked after your interests?"

"Sometimes too well. What is it this time? No friends to talk to?"

"Oh no, I just finished putting together this incredible stained-glass piece and wanted to show you. Here."

The giant monitor pixelates briefly then goes black. Julia's voice loses its inherent sweetness and reverberates forcefully through the monitor rim. "Roger, have you changed your 3D graphics software on me again?"

"Do I have to tell you every time I make a change Julia? Increase your resolution to at least 7,680 x 4,320 or it won't show. I need precision in my work, so I've upgraded my settings."

"OK, OK, I understand." Calmer now. "But you don't have to be snotty hon. Give me a minute while I find the original version."

Impatient, Roger starts typing again. The work must be completed in the next hour or he'll lose all credibility, and possibly a man's life. The doctors at the remote war-zone hospital are waiting for his suggested procedure while the soldier has been put into a short-acting freeze-coma. Why does his ex-wife bug him at crucial times? Is it always coincidence?   The Artificial Intelligence (AI) programs monitoring his activity are supposed to be highly secure, but he wonders. Does she know someone in the Information Technology panel at the institute, or has a random AI tentacle drawn some new conclusions?

His screen bursts into vibrant color, and the monitor rotates to a portrait position. A posie of beautiful springtime flowers fills a window frame with a rounded top. The blossoms glow in streaks of golden sunlight. A subtle fragrance accompanies the presentation. The image is so real Roger feels he could touch it. He starts to reach forward then pulls back.

"It's out of this world, Julia. Absolutely stunning. Is it for a virtual chapel you're helping design?"

"Glad you like it. And yes. Even here with the multitude of choices available to architects I still have something others don't. Are you proud of me?"

"Always have been. Happy that your talent and craftsmanship haven't deserted you. And I see your modesty hasn't changed either."

"There you go, being snotty again. I don't <u>have</u> to share my accomplishments with you you know."

Roger mumbles "Sometimes less would be more."

"Oh, come on, you'd be ever so lonely if I didn't pop in once in a while. And by the way I have some other news to share although I doubt you'll appreciate it."

"Get it out then. I need to finish my video. Can you make it quick?"

"Always in a hurry. I think that's what killed me in the end. Haste!" The monitor goes black, then the outline of a hissing devil is superimposed over the beautiful flowers. Swirls of tendrils rip into the flower stems and the petals become crippled and smashed. A burning smell accompanies the image.

"Stop it, Julia. That's not fair. I did my best. My colleagues did their best. You were gone, Julia, you were gone. There was no way to stop the slide you were on. No way."

"I don't know if I'll ever believe you Roger."

"How many times can I tell you. We did not hurry your death for the transplant organs. That would be totally against hospital policy. Why do you keep bringing it up? You always forget that two teenage girls lived because of your generosity. And you never seem to understand what it took out of me to see you die under my hands as we all tried our hardest to save you. I don't need this. I'm turning my screen off. Goodbye." He pushes the nodule in his throat and voices, "Control. Close monitor." The screen's low hum dies and fades to nothing.

Roger shakes his head, taps the pad on the arm of his mobile chair, and selects coffee from the menu on the transparent 3D holo-image that rises. It bugs him that he can't verbally-activate this particular coffee maker model. As the machine switches on, Julia's voice emanates from the cup holder in the chair's arm. "Alright, alright, I'm sorry. I really do hate not being able to help myself. Then and now. But I died too young Roger."

Momentarily Roger remembers the debilitating hurt he experienced after Julia's death. His heart ached for a good two years. For one who saw a hospital death nearly every week he couldn't handle his own wife's passing. It was two long years before a comrade induced a smile. But at some point, living with himself started to get easier. Accepting Julia's avatar into his life was a major step forward. There were times it was comforting. Others when it wasn't. Interactive only in his home, he could avoid it by being absent. He wondered if he should leave now. The emergency assignment would never get completed if he did however.

"I know Julia. I know. Now what else were you going to tell me? You mentioned some other information. I won't like it?"

"Probably not. It's about that woman you had dinner with last night. No, no, no, wait. I see the scowl forming on your face. I understand your need for physical companionship. I really do. But Janine? She's a gold digger Roger. I've done some checking. Information you can't get access to. Way beyond her standard persona background details."

"What sort of details Julia? For crying out loud, last night was the first time I met her. Pretty, smart, self-confident, well-travelled, some common interests. Was nice to meet someone easy to converse with. No kids, owns an upscale condo. So what? No commitments to follow-up on either side. We may never even see each other again."

"I assure you she wasn't honest with some of her tales. If you do follow-up, ask for more information about how she got to be VP at her work-place. Not through performance and creativity, let me tell you."

"Sometimes you really irritate me Julia. Must you snoop every time I interact with the opposite sex. At work, at play, wherever? I don't ask you about other avatar relationships. Are you jealous of my freedom?"

"Just trying to protect you dear. You are getting testy again."

"Either pass on what you know, or leave me alone please."

"Ok, you asked for it. Your new girlfriend is lesbian. No sex there hon. And I appreciate that sex is still a part of your life.

Virtual sex is part of our lives here too. But if real sex was anywhere on your mind, may as well throw it away now."

"Geez Julia, you are really pissing me off. I could care less. She's just a nice lady. What's wrong? Are you unhappy these days?"

"Just remembering your interests dear. I can send some hot stuff to your monitor if you like that might make up for missed opportunities."

Back in the study the monitor snaps to life. Orgasmic groans fill the small nook where Roger sips his coffee. He refuses to look back at the screen. He turns his face and speaks to the table lamp.

"if you were here in person Julia, I'd throw this coffee over you. It's clearly time to ease down your visitation rights. You're becoming obnoxious. I thought they'd removed that future menopause crap from your system, but I guess not. Go work on some more art pieces and keep yourself distracted. And quit playing with my monitor. Turn it off."

"Touchy man. Are you forgetting all the good times we had together? It's only been four years you know."

"Is there some virtual-participation test you've failed Julia? Communication never was your forte. I thought they'd examined all those downloads from the internet showing past thoughts, behavior, and practices, and minimized their impact in the future you. Maybe it's my fault for not paying the extra fee to make sure you got the superior transfer service, instead of the regular one."

"You know, I still miss you Roger. Can we go horse-riding together again? Along the cliff-top with the wind in my hair and the scent of the pine trees all around? That was the best vacation ever. Even if it was my last one. I can set it all up. All you need to do is put your Virtual Reality set on and sit in the easy chair."

"Are you sure you want to do that Julia? Maybe just the short fun part at the start. It didn't work well in the end as you are aware. We need to stop before the accident. OK? I desperately need to dictate my procedure for the surgery video I'm making."

"Oh good, good, good. See, sometimes we can still have fun together Roger. I'll be with you shortly. Wait for your system to buzz. Here it comes."

***   ***   ***

Roger smiles as he feels the breeze blowing on his face, and hears the surf whispering against the rocks at the bottom of the cliff. Julia is riding ahead of him, happy and carefree. Out of the corner of his eye he sees the snake slithering in the grass. He yells a warning but it's too late. As Julia's horse rears up, blackness envelops Roger in a crushing embrace. He tears the headset off and howls like a banshee. His hands tremble as he stands and holds the hologram of Julia's broken body across his outstretched arms. Thrown onto the rocks by her frightened horse, his warning and control were too late once more. She had promised to stop, but she lied again.

Tears flow hard, and he curses out loud. He looks down at her beautiful face, framed with the golden locks he loved so much. "You'll never believe me will you Julia? Never. You want me to suffer your death over and over. You even made a gorgeous chapel window for your farewell service. Will you never truly say goodbye?"

V is for Victory

The LED-powered heads-up display on the car's windshield flashes off and on three times, indicating a new external source trying to make contact and take control. Simultaneously the data that had been showing on the window resolves to the onboard nav-info screen, replacing the map there. It is a very selective group of robots to which I have given permission to interrupt me this way.

A sultry voice sounds urgently in my hearing implants. It's the female director of the holding facility where my ex-wife's avatar is stored. "Attention prime guardian. Inmate six nine slash zero five dash twenty thirty-five has eluded facility surveillance and may try to make contact. This is a warning. We are here to serve. Respond 'more' in three seconds if you desire extra detail."

I sigh but don't respond. "Damn, she's out again," I mutter out loud. "I wonder where she's headed this time." I reach to the in-dash screen and activate the services module. "Locate six nine slash zero five dash twenty thirty five, and hover. Do not engage." A muted tone assures me that my command has been accepted. I drum my fingers on the simulated steering wheel as the driverless car veers carefully across two lanes of heavy traffic in anticipation of using an exit 400 hundred yards ahead. It slows smoothly from the 160 kph it's been travelling at along the expensive overhead transit lanes, in order to join the cross-town guide route to my lawyer's office. I wonder if Campbell, the name I've selected for my life-aware system, will locate my ex-wife before I arrive.

It doesn't happen. I'll just have to deal with ex-wife later.

Inside the legal office I let my anger show. "Amazing coincidence, or maybe not so. She's a vixen Phil. Escapes again just as I'm on my way to talk to you about her."

"This is what, the third time Alex? How does she do it?"

"Haven't I told you before? That facility she's in is managed by Cray's latest super computer. It's serendipity for her, as she used to be the head programmer at Cray, before she went rogue. How she was placed at that facility and not elsewhere is unbelievable. I sometimes wonder if it really was coincidence or rather, that she influenced the decision somehow. The girl with the dragon tattoo looks like a hacker apprentice compared to Cassandra."

"I thought we'd done all we could to protect you Alex. What's new?"

"You mean aside from her current little adventure? I bet she'll be found in a city hall somewhere, trying to access records to find my trail again. I need some new ideas Phil. Here, let me share my updated life-aware system file."

I stand, reach in through my pants pocket and withdraw the thumbnail-sized nano-wafer from the man-made sleeve in my scrotum. I place it on the pad on Phil's desk and press my thumb and forefinger on the attached screen when requested. A soft fan noise is the only indication that the sixty terabytes of information are being copied to the lawyer's depository.

"I want you to have one of your cyber experts check whether there's some weakness in my life-aware security system that she may be able to exploit. I want to get on with my new life Phil, not be constantly looking over my shoulder to see what Cass is doing now. The thought police have caught up with her in fast order on the last two escapes. I suspect this time it will take them longer. She's after more of my assets, although she can't use them readily in her deceased state."

"Why would she want more then Alex? I don't get it."

"There's new information in my life-aware system file Phil. I'm being pursued by a woman who claims I'm the father of her son and she needs more support now he is in college. Frankly I don't remember her. I've racked my brain, and challenged her claim, but she's threatening a very public DNA-humiliation campaign. You know what those are like. She's resisting providing non-DNA proof of our liaison."

"And you have no memory of her Alex? Really?"

"Look, like you and a million other guys, sex was a way of life when I was in college. For girls as well as us guys. Nothing like a thick dick in a slick mick, right? I had my v-cectomy the first day I could legally make it happen – two days after graduation from High School. No more latex phallus covers. I hated those things. Felt like taking a shower with my boots on.

"This woman says she got pregnant real soon after we met, but won't give me dates. Her name, Vanessa, rings no bells. She must have fake dates from a hospital's delivery unit and reversed conception records, but obviously won't tell me the name of the hospital. I'm beginning to wonder if my ex-wife is involved with her, trying to find some other way into my life-aware system files. Which is why I want your cyber help. A real woman collaborating with my ex's avatar. Oh yes, to add fuel to my suspicions, this woman claims she was a computer science student. Can't imagine what we had in common beyond good old banging, as I was an arts major. Something odd going on here."

"OK then, we'll be happy to give your system a major security check-over Alex. Might take my folks 24 hours. Experience suggests we'll probably find some surprises. I have an important trial appearance tomorrow morning so I'll call you in the afternoon."

***   ***   ***

On return to my road transport machine I find the heads-up display indicating the search for my ex-wife's avatar has been successful. A flashing message indicates I should contact Security at Cayman Island Bank urgently. My own bank! What the heck is going on? I hit the save/transfer/act button on my wristband control unit and the call is automatically initiated with the dial tone registering in my hearing chips. Once authentication has been established I am transferred to the underground Trust department where a kind voice says, "How may I help you Mr. Robinson?"

"I understand my ex-wife's avatar has made contact, sir. Can you confirm please?"

"That is indeed correct sir. She's resident in her friend's personal electronic display purse, and the two recently entered the vault."

"She has someone with her?"

"Yes sir, a Vanessa Wainright. Your wife had all the appropriate credentials sir, including the number and status of your security lock box. And Ms. Wainright's identity tabs check out perfectly sir. She has a J-5 clearance level."

"Good heavens. This is unbelievable. Let me double check arrangements with you sir. Has anyone else visited the Trust department seeking access to my trust drawer since I was last there?"

"No Mr. Robinson. No one."

"So the women have the hardware passwords and material to open the drawer. Correct?"

"Yes, sir."

"But this is the new graphene hardware/encryption combination arrangements invented by the CIA right? Developed to secretly hide President Trump's personal data 30 years ago in order to thwart the liberals' efforts aimed at delegitimizing him."

"You have an excellent memory sir. That technology is applied to all boxes in our trust department now. Has been for twenty years since it was initially commercialized. At some stage you must have shared your passwords with your then wife sir, I imagine. I did notice that the unlock device her friend, Ms. Wainright, had, was only recently certified by the national security standards bureau. It looked brand-new."

"Ok, so much for the 3D printed unlock device. The actual trust computing machine inside the security box is still present though, correct? The nuclear battery that powers it hasn't failed I presume?"

"True sir. Unless you disconnected it, although we'd probably know that had happened."

"I left everything where it was. And all trust machines now have 1024-bit encryption right?"

"Yes sir. You have to have a sequence of 10 different passwords to gain access to any files and to activate online connections."

"And have the ladies gained access to my files?"

"I wouldn't know that sir. They are in a private room."

"OK, I appreciate all you've told me. Thank you for your patience."

"Nothing more Mr. Robinson? Should I let the ladies know you were checking?"

"Please don't. You might find them to be a little frustrated when they exit, as I deleted all files on that machine when I last visited. Goodbye."

I mutter to myself. 'Just as I thought. Cassandra's avatar has been working overtime to get to my assets. She has the location of the files and the passwords, and she's pulled in a potential enemy of her enemy, me, to do the physical work. That explains all too well why I haven't heard from her in so long. It's clearly time to move things along and silence her for good.'

Early the next morning I'm surprised to get a phone call from the lawyer's office. "This is Chris, Mr. Robinson. I've been examining your life-aware system and have found two breaches in the lowest level of your security layers. One is serious. First, in the lesser case, someone very smart has hacked the area in your system that searches across all public and semi-private databases for any contacts you've made. The last search looked back over twenty-five years. Must have taken all night or used a super computer to come up with a bunch of findings. If you'll excuse me sir, it looks like the search retrieved a bunch of female names along with certain attributes and qualifications of each person. Some are a bit embarrassing Mr. Robinson. I can forward the list to you if you want, although I should warn you there's nearly 250 entries."

"Oh my. My past is catching up with me. Let me guess. One of the names is Vanessa Wainright? Am I correct?"

"Yes sir. Would you like me to read whatever notes you included?"

"I suppose I'm about to die of shame, but go ahead. I was just another macho jock at college twenty-five years ago. I've just learned this woman is working with my ex-wife's avatar trying to steal information from my security lock-box, and most likely is the one who has separately accused me of fathering a son of hers. I sure don't remember her, but maybe the notes will help me recollect."

"Actually, there's not that much written here at all sir, unlike other entries. Just two words, a set of initials and a number. 'Velvet vulva, VVV. 8/10.' Does that jog the memory at all?"

I don't hesitate more than 2 seconds. "It sure does. Oh boy, now I remember her. Vanessa VV. We used to joke about the three Vs. My secret nickname for her in public. Vanessa VV. Long time ago for sure. She had features and capabilities others could only dream about. How on earth could I have forgotten her?"

"Well, I've closed that loophole for you Mr. Robinson, and we'll apply what we've learned to all our other clients' life-aware systems. In a way we thank you for having us make this check-up.

"And I hate to tell you, but the other issue we found has implications that are more profound. It took some very heavy-duty test algorithms to isolate this bug. Whoever hacked your life-system now knows the locations of your security boxes and the passwords for access."

I swear beneath my breath. "I guessed as much Chris. I received an urgent message yesterday afternoon concerning third party entities accessing my security box at the local Cayman Island Bank branch. Luckily that's one of my 3 decoys. But it means I have to act shortly in order to protect the real box. You've inadvertently given me an idea. Maybe I can come in and talk to you and Phil about it this afternoon?"

"Fine by me. I look forward to your visit. When Phil is finished with online court I'll tell him to expect you."

I ruminate on my idea over lunch, feeling satisfied that it will work.

***   ***   ***

Chris has filled Phil in on the cyber threats and has brought several strangers into the conference room. They are not introduced. Phil says, "Don't we need to hurry Alex? No doubt Cassandra is already planning to check out the other safe boxes. She could be at your primary location even as we speak."

"Yes, and no Phil. We have a little time."

"But she knows your passwords. You can't change them immediately. Once through the final hurdle and online she can start transferring assets to her accounts."

"The 'no' part of my response has to do with those passwords. You see, I've added an extra password once inside my primary box. I hired a world class hacker who accompanied me on my last visit to the bank and found a way to add code to the bank's application. It now requires an extra password for access to the core information. I have no doubt Cassandra will realize what's going on when she finally finds the primary box, but she'll have to go back to her Cray and write her own routine to search for the eleventh password when she returns a second time to my box."

"Pretty smart Alex. Certainly will slow her down. Chris says you have a new idea however. Please share it."

"It came to me when I was thinking about all those V initials Chris discovered. I'd like to devise a 'Venus fly-trap' for both Cassandra and her new friend Vanessa. I need to hire my hacker again unless one of your folks is willing to do some coding."

Chris has brought in more of his cyber team, I guess. I look around the room and see several smiles. Any one of the programmers present would like to strut their stuff.

"Well," Chris stammers. "Sometimes we stretch the interpretation of legal limits by employing a friendly grey-market company to do 'dark-work' for us. The extra people around the table work for that company, which will remain nameless, as will they. We thought it might be useful to have them here."

I turn to the group. "Ah, that explains why I've never seen you all before. Thanks for coming."

"Ok, so explain your idea to us."

"I will use legitimate currency entries and transfers to make one of my accounts stand out in dollar volume by a magnitude of twenty relative to all the other accounts. That will spring the trap. My bet is that Cassandra is paying Vanesa a small commission for her human access involvement. So they will split the total amount in my account and make two transfers, the larger one, I'd guess at least 90%, to Cassandra's avatar account at her facility, the rest to Vanessa's account.

"What I'm looking for is a simple switch arrangement. Once Cassandra enters their two account numbers and the split ratio, the trap closes. When she clicks on the 'Transfer' button, instead of moving funds out of my account, the new hack drains both their accounts into mine. A message simply indicates 'Transfer in progress'. Finally, their screen should show 'Transfers complete' when done. At that point the hack makes a small change in the original tenth access password, which we'll agree in advance, and the system shuts down totally. Think that could work?"

Thumbs go up all around the room, and one of the young women asks, "Can you provide us with a copy of the code your hacker used to set up the eleventh password? I think if we have that we can do what you want in pretty short order."

***   ***   ***

Ten days have passed and I'm on a plane heading to Turks and Caicos in the Caribbean. I'm flying first class on one of the new supersonic jets and loving it. A call registers in my eardrums and a sterile announcement indicates it's Cassandra's avatar.

"You bastard Alex. At least you could have left me a little something. Now I almost have to beg for food money. No-one here will use my hacking capabilities thanks to your little escapade to outsmart me. I hate you with all of my fake heart. Even my new friend Vanessa has deserted me. She doesn't respond to my contact efforts. Do you know where she is?"

I answer with a smirk across my face. "V is for victory my dear. Goodbye."

I shut off the connection, lean back contentedly, and turn to my companion. I smile as Vanessa sensually glides her playful fingers down inside the front of her panties.

Foot-Fault

Despite the nylon sheathing on the fence surrounding the two tennis courts, the wind still created random eddies back and forth across the nets. I watched carefully to see if it really was the wind wreaking havoc on the soft-touch shots, or whether it was Bill's avatar playing games with me and my partner again. The occasion was the mixed doubles final, and Sherrie and I were battling it out with Bruce and Cassandra. We were nearing the end of the second set.

Something was wrong, I was convinced. The last drop-shot my wife attempted had fallen just short of the net. It was one of her signature shots, usually a guaranteed winner with its delicate backspin, and she rarely missed it. It meant I was now down 30-40 on my serve, and I wasn't happy. I was pretty sure Bill's avatar was influencing matters. My mind wasn't concentrating on the game like it should and I served a fault to Cassie. Her forehand was her best weapon so I lined up my second serve to her backhand. It was a good serve, deep, and with a slight slice moving away due to my left-handed delivery. I followed in a few steps although I was really anticipating an unreturnable result. Amazingly, an uncharacteristically strong backhand shot came screaming back. Sherrie, bless her heart, was ready. She moved quickly to her left to poach midcourt and I saw her make solid contact with the ball. It was headed down the centerline for a sure winner, but it hit the tape at the top of the net and fell back. Once again, I was stunned. So was Sherrie. She just doesn't miss shots like that. I was now sure that Bill's avatar was busy thwarting our efforts.

Our opponents had just won the second set, so it was one set apiece, and the four of us were in the clubhouse downing cool drinks. Bruce was gracious. "You let us off with those two misses Sherrie. Very unlike you, but thanks anyway." Sherrie smiled but said nothing. She looked at me and I nodded. We both knew what had happened. At that moment, Bill's voice emanated from the base of the doubles winner's trophy sitting on the back shelf. "Come on Stan and Sherrie. That was a bit unlucky, but you have a third set still to play. It looks very even. I'm enjoying watching."

I tried to be friendly with my response. "Just make sure you keep quiet during the next set Bill, I heard you laughing during the early part of that last set. Neither team needs your distractions."

"Laughing?" Bill responded. "You're right, there was more to laugh about than to applaud in those games. You missed a couple of simple overheads if you remember,"

Bruce breaks in. "Pipe down Bill." Just 'cause you no longer play doesn't mean you can still try to be an expert with your opinions. We know the Trophy sits there because of your donation, but try to be a spectator enjoying the game, rather than an analyst commenting for some newspaper report."

No response from Bill.

Bruce's input was very appropriate. Its relevance allows me to give you some more background on what the current match is all about. Bear with me.

***   ***   ***

When the condominium tower was complete and all the new residents had moved in, it was Bill who had taken a survey and found eighteen over-fifty folks who'd be interested in forming a small tennis club to play on the rooftop courts. The building's developer had been a good tennis player when younger and had added the two courts for a nominal upcharge to the price of each condo unit.

Bill emerged as an enthusiastic leader who arranged a visiting instructor/coach once a week, got the Penn company to donate cartons of balls, secured the two court nets at wholesale prices, and arranged for the local sports store to donate two squeegees and brooms.

One of the building's tenants was an architect who drew up a plan for a simple one-room shaded outdoor clubhouse, and arranged the building permit. Another non-playing tenant donated the lumber at wholesale prices, and each team member donated $500 to cover expenses. For $10,000 the group ended up with a simple weatherproof shelter with two bench seats, each seating three, a table to hold drinks and hors d'oeuvres or playing cards, and a small refrigerator for ice-cold beverages. At $20 maintenance per month the facility offered great value, and the group members loved its functionality.

It was during the first mixed doubles tournament that instances of bickering arose. Eight teams had formed, and play times were established by mutual agreement. Bill, who was the tallest and strongest, but not the best player, was accused of deliberately picking some of the windiest times to play, his bulk and speed being less affected by the wind than were others with different builds. The event nearly failed when one couple refused to play him and his partner, Sandra, at the end of one day when the offshore winds drove across the city with considerable force. My friend, Bruce, helped create a compromise arrangement for an earlier time on the following day and even offered to referee the match.

Bill's drive and commitment could become a little overbearing at times. Rather than suggesting ways other members could improve their games he'd berate them, admittedly in a relatively gentle way, for missing an easy shot or serving a double fault. And when he committed an inexcusable error of his own volition, it was never his fault, 'the ball bounced funny', 'the sun was in my eyes', 'someone in the clubhouse spoke just as I went to hit', 'my palm was sweaty', etc. His general enthusiasm, his high energy in keeping the courts clean, and his willingness to organize matches were well respected. If only he could be a little more personable when playing, he'd have more friends.

Everyone else tolerated Bill's inputs better than I did.

I was probably the best singles player in the group, winning two-thirds of my matches against Bill, despite his size and strength. Bruce matched Bill evenly and was more fun for me to play, as he was always happy to be enjoying the game. The two of us worked hard to counter Bill's unnecessary earnestness wherever we could, ably helped by our wives. Bruce was friendlier than I was, as I simply found Bill's constant comments irritating. Bruce could let more of them drip off his back than I could. Bill knew it and worked hard at throwing barbs my way.

To give credit to his generosity, Bill was praised for purchasing a small symbolic trophy for the annual doubles tournament, which Bruce and Cassandra won in a tightly fought final against me and Sherrie last year. We were out for revenge this time around.

***   ***   ***

The biggest problem with the courts was the wind. Thirty floors above ground the wind was present about one third of the days, varying in strength with the temperature and humidity. A higher than usual wire fence surrounded the two courts, approximately twenty feet tall, the bottom half of which was wrapped with heavy nylon to minimize the winds' effects.

It was Bill who suggested that wrapping the top half of the fence would make playing conditions even more enjoyable for everyone. He suggested that a small donation from each member would cover costs. Most folks agreed.

On the second day of the new installation, one of the workers failed to turn up. In the spirit of helping out, Bill offered to take his place. I was present and urged Bill not to act in haste. In my view this was a dangerous job, best left to experts. And to cap it all there was a mild wind blowing. Bill called me a wimp and criticized me for not wanting to also help.

"All you want are the benefits of wind protection, Stan. You could care less about helping provide them. This is a man's job. If you aren't up to it, maybe you don't belong here anymore. All you do is criticize whatever I try to offer something to the facility. I'm tired of you and your thanklessness. I do everything to make our club a pleasure to be part of. But whenever I open my mouth you are there with some sort of comeback. Why don't you leave so we real men can get this job done!"

He seemed angrier than I'd seen him in a while. I found out later that he and his wife, Sandra, who was younger by twenty years, had had a nasty argument earlier that morning, in which Bill had accused her of cheating on him with the coach, Roger, who came in weekly.

Frankly, I'd seen some unusual coaching arrangements between student and teacher, especially when he held her arm to illustrate how a stroke should be played. And she tended to wear lower cut blouses and shorter skirts in her lessons than when she played doubles against us. She was petite, and pretty, but I put her down as a prick-tease, and really didn't care for her. Being a somewhat chauvinistic male, however, I will admit I loved seeing her breasts bounce up and down, and to sometimes be rewarded after a wind gust with the sight of a bonus sexy camel-toe in the front of her panties.

It made sense that Bill's and my argument about not helping with the windscreen installation may have left Bill less focused than usual, but after yelling at me, he climbed one of the ladders and helped attach the nylon sheet to the top of the wire fence.

I was about to head back inside when suddenly I heard a scream and turned around only to see Bill falling backwards onto the parapet around the rooftop. He was clearly in agony, bones surely broken. As the two workers and I rushed to his aid he moaned horribly and the bulk of his body started sliding over the edge of the concrete bulwark. In a frantic reach I managed to grab his shoe as he screamed again.

"Stan, hold me, hold me," he yelled, but his foot was sliding out of his shoe. As I made a desperate lunge for his ankle with my other hand, the shoe came totally off, his leg twisted, and I was left groping empty air. I felt a worker grab me from behind and add some stability but it didn't take my view away as I watched Bill smash into the visitors' parking lot hundreds of feet below and lie very still, a pool of blood starting to form at his side near his neck.

***   ***   ***

I was miserable for weeks afterwards, wondering if I could have done more to prevent the accident. I apologized over and over to Sandra, who was surprisingly gracious in her response. "I know you and Bill had differences, Stan, but he often said he had no real long-term grudge against you.

Rather wished he could play as well as you. Please try to forgive yourself. From what the workmen said there was nothing extra or different you could have done. They regretted they hadn't been closer to where Bill was working to have been able to help out. And don't worry about me. I will survive."

People take the death of a mate in different ways. There are all those theories about stages of recovery that the survivor must go through. I had a feeling that Sandra simply didn't fit the usual model, because a week after Bill's funeral she arranged another lesson. The new screening was in place and the courts were empty except for the basket of balls Roger used in his lessons. Surprisingly, it had been left in the center of the court. I wheeled it back to its usual parking spot as Roger emerged from the roof door. He was a mess. His shirt was hanging loose, his hair was mussed, and he was carrying his shoes and socks.

"Roger," I queried. "What happened?" It dawned on me as he replied. "The lady said she needed to be held, so I obliged, as she seemed so sad. Things escalated and it became clear she needed more than just a hug. Let me tell you, she's an absolute tiger in bed."

Not my place to make judgments, but Sandra's actions weren't that big a surprise. I kept the information to myself, although I noticed she soon extended her lessons from sixty to ninety minutes and spent the extra time with Roger in her unit 'chatting about strategy', as she explained it to us. Pigs wallop, as they say.

Sandra had arranged to have Bill's avatar created and organized per one of his wishes. He'd retired early after an exemplary career at an advanced systems electronics company which specialized in fire-line technological defence materials, and about which he could reveal very little due to his government clearance levels. From snippets of input into various discussion areas it was clear however that he was a highly sophisticated scientist working at the fore-front of electronic and material nano technology.

***   ***   ***

In the clubhouse, Bill's voice brought me back from memories with a reminder. "OK, you've had five minutes' break folks. Time to get back out on the court again and finish this match." His avatar voice emanating from the trophy again. During the rest period I'd been thinking more about the potential for Bill to interfere. A new thought had entered my brain. My wife's two significant shots that failed were around the net. Could it be that Bill had established a schema whereby extra wires, magnets or other nano sources could have been embedded in the net allowing him through sound waves or otherwise to impact the path of a tennis ball nearby? He was the one who had purchased the nets, although I remember it took longer than I would have expected to arrange delivery. Was I being paranoid in thinking the mesh netting had some secret components we lay people would never know about?

I knew nothing about high-falutin' electronic technology. I was a sailor with a captain's license. The closest I got to technology was managing to interpret the information on the various screens in my boat's pilothouse. The only thing I knew that was obvious to everyone was that all the instruments on the boat needed electricity to run.

Ha, maybe that was the secret on our tennis courts.

We had lights for evening matches if folks wanted to play after dark. In such instances they paid a fee to offset the cost of the powerful lights. At the back of our shelter there was a panel of electronic breakers that was rarely touched. As the others filed back out to the court I opened the panel and flipped the master switch to off. I was rewarded with an "Oof, what?" exclamation from the trophy base, and then silence. At least I'd shut Bill up, a small victory in itself.

It was the fourth game of the deciding set before there was any chance to test my theory about third-party 'net-influence'. Sherrie was running forward to a weak shot from Cassandra that had landed short in the service box. Both Bruce and Cassandra were near the baseline, providing a perfect opportunity for Sherrie to try her drop-shot. Which she did.

It worked perfectly.

Gave me renewed confidence, and as a result, I played some of my better tennis. It helped us win the set six games to two. Meaning, this year the trophy would be ours. The four of us shook hands across the net and headed back to the shelter to collect our belongings and return to our individual home units downstairs. I flipped the electricity master breaker switch back on just as Bruce asked loudly "Where have you been Bill? Didn't hear a peep out of you during that set. You're usually giving one of the teams advice. Cat got your tongue today?"

There was a sharp buzzing sound from the base of the trophy, after which Bill's voice came through loud and clear. "Some technical difficulties with the network caused a hiccup Bruce. Sorry about that. I've just gotten back in touch. Who won the match?"

"Stan and Sherrie got the better of us today Bill. So the trophy honors them until next year."

"Hmmm, I'm a little surprised given the difficulty Sherrie was having in the last game of that second set."

"No sign of any issues in the deciding set at all. Such a pity you weren't here to get images of the match. Surely your avatar has some from the event. You can access those when you have time."

Bill sounded pouty. "I might do that sometime."

I grabbed the trophy to put on our mantle shelf and we invited Bruce and Cassandra to come and have dinner with us in an hour's time, an invitation they graciously accepted. We weren't that competitive that we couldn't stay friends.

When they arrived Bruce asked "Where's the trophy Stan? I expected to see it as a centerpiece on the dining room table."

I smiled. "In my haste to collar it, Bruce, I left its base in the shelter and it can't stand up on its own. I'll go get it after dinner. No problem. Might be nicer with its absence anyway."

***   ***   ***

I took the elevator to the rooftop, and the second I walked into the hut Bill's voice accosted me. "You never did like me did you Stan? You're the one who turned off the power when you played that last set. I'm sure of it. Just to spite me so I couldn't see the match."

"Bill, you are being a pain in the ass. I turned it off to see if magnetic waves from the power arrangement were having an influence on the game somehow. Sherrie's soft shots definitely improved that last set."

"You think you are so smart Stan. But you're not in the same league as me. I've had the knowledge on how to make magnetic waves and impulses distort atom patterns in real objects for years. The company I worked for researched how to turn that knowledge into advanced combat weaponry. We were incredibly successful. In fact I've deployed some of our findings right here on the roof. For example, if a ball gets close enough to the net I can grab it electronically and move it wherever I want. Scary huh?"

The man had just confirmed my supposition. I hoped he'd keep 'educating' me. Sure enough he couldn't refrain from boasting further. "As for that young whippersnapper, Roger, Sandra's coach, he has no idea what I can see and hear in our old unit. Sandra is a nymphomaniac of the first order. Something I certainly benefited from admittedly. But Roger has no maturity or class, just a mammoth dick. I've been experimenting with how I can affect its performance. Next coaching session both of them are in for an unexpected surprise, and it won't be laughable or repeatable, believe me. His and her fumbling inabilities will be broadcast real-time over the Internet. You won't believe how many folks have queued up and already paid to watch what will happen.""

"Bill, I really don't want to hear about your technological prowess. It's clear you are self-centered and don't care about others...."

He interrupts me. "Your memory is a little short Stan. Who was it who set up the club here, arranged the clubhouse, got all the equipment together and wrapped the incredibly tall fence to keep the wind out. No one has matched what I've done for everyone else."

"We all give you credit there, Bill, but, personally, I expect if we were to hire someone whose intellect and talent matched yours we'd actually find all those things you bought are riddled with sensors, information gatherers, and extraneous probes and nano needles designed to 'spy' on the rest of us and be used against us according to your whims."

"Close, Stan, close. Maybe there's hope for you yet. I'd give you some leeway but it's clear you never cared for me. Even when I fell off the roof, I knew you wouldn't hold me securely and try to prevent my fall. You've disliked me from day one, because you felt threatened by all I did for tennis while you stood meekly by."

"You're welcome to keep deluding yourself Bill. I've told you before, I did all I could to stop you falling. I wish I could have saved you, I honestly do, but it wasn't to happen. Despite your arrogance in trying to prove yourself better than the rest of us by offering to help out, I did not shirk in trying to rescue you. No way. It's a totally unfair accusation to lay on me. Typical of your ungraciousness."

"You grabbed my shoe, not my ankle or leg at first. Why not grab an integral part of me? I know the answer in case you don't. You just didn't care enough to want to do it."

"You're starting to really irritate me Bill. How many times do I have to tell you that all of us here regret your horrible accident. To suggest I didn't try to help however is an insult of the first order. And I'm tired of this conversation. I tried to save you. I'm amazed you are so unthankful."

I scratch my head. What is wrong with this chap? What am I supposed to do? Before I can think of something, he starts in again.

"I actually wonder if you deliberately didn't hold my ankle tight enough and deliberately let me drop Stan. Somehow, one day I will get even. My little control center up here will have its revenge. Just you wait."

An unexpected brain wave pokes into my analytic thinking center. I pick up the base of the trophy and raise it high over my head. I talk to it directly. "Never thought about it before, but this must be your so-called avatar control center Bill. Right under our very noses. You should never have mentioned it old chap. I would never have suspected."

"So what? You can't do anything with it Stan. It's under my control, not yours. And it's an integral part of the Trophy. Just leave it on the shelf there."

My brain and heart have a visceral reaction. NO FLAMING WAY! No sir, not on your life.

I quickly walk around the perimeter of the roof to the spot where Bill fell. I don't hesitate. I hurl the trophy base as hard as I can into the night ether, watch it float all the way to the ground where it smashes into little pieces. Bill's avatar is no more, at least on our rooftop.

It's gone. Bill is gone. Peace will reign on the tennis courts.

Which leaves only one more decision to make.

Do I tell Sandra what her ex-husband plans to do, or do I let Roger and her hang in the wind?

I'll decide tomorrow.... Might depend on what she's wearing for her morning lesson.....